AF413481

My Family Reconnection Blueprint

A Trauma-Informed Framework for Healing, Accountability, and Lasting Bonds.

Jessie Mikes

Copyright

Copyright © 2026 Jessie Mikes

Published by

Dedication

This book is dedicated to my family, whose unwavering love and support have been the foundation of this journey. To my parents, who taught me perseverance and compassion; to my friends, who believed in me when I doubted; and to my late great brother **Ajabu** — whose steadiness, stories, and fierce love continue to guide every step I take toward reconnection.

Epigraph

"Repair is an art; patience and steady hands mend what's been torn."

Disclaimer

The information and exercises in this workbook are provided for educational and self-help purposes only and do not constitute professional legal, medical, psychological, or therapeutic advice. Readers should consult qualified professionals for guidance specific to their circumstances. The author and publisher make no warranties regarding the suitability or results of any exercises and disclaim liability for outcomes arising from use of this workbook. If you are experiencing a legal emergency, medical crisis, or serious mental-health concern, seek immediate help from a licensed professional or local emergency services.

Note on Case Studies

Case studies and stories are included solely to illustrate lessons and practical approaches to family reconnection. Identifying details such as names, locations, ages, and occupations have been changed to protect privacy. Some examples are composites drawn from multiple real situations; others are based on first-person accounts shared with explicit consent, and those instances are noted in the text. These narratives are illustrative and should not be interpreted as documentation of any specific individual's circumstances.

Table of Contents

Part I: FOUNDATIONS OF RECONNECTION 8
LESSON 1: Introduction..................................9

LESSON 2: Recognizing Your Moment of Truth................... 19

LESSON 3: Step One Accountability as the Gateway to Healing 26

Part II The Blueprint Framework 32
LESSON 4: Consistency Builds Trust *The Power of Reliability*...........33

LESSON 5: *The Custodial Parent's Role* 39

LESSON 6: The Children's Inner World 45

LESSON 7: Communication Bridges 52

Part III Tools for Family & Professionals 57
LESSON 8: Bonding Anew..............................58

LESSON 9: Co-Parenting in Practice 64

LESSON 10: Designing the Reconnection Plan................70

PART IV - Maintaining the Journey....................77
LESSON 11: Weathering Setbacks........................78

LESSON 12: Celebrating Wins 84

LESSON 13: A Stronger Tomorrow 91

Acknowledgments 99

A Final Word...................................100

RESOURCES & REFERENCES.......................101

GLOSSARY....................................102

ABOUT THE AUTHOR 103

Part I:
FOUNDATIONS OF RECONNECTION

LESSON 1:
Introduction

Charting the Course to Reconnection

Welcome to My Family Reconnection Blueprint: A Trauma-Informed Framework for Healing, Accountability, and Lasting Bonds. I am Jessie Mikes, and I have devoted my career to guiding families through the painful separations life can bring.

Today, you hold more than a workbook—you hold a compass for healing. It is built from real courtroom experience and a deep conviction that every broken bond can be mended.

As a reunification, visitation, and anger management professional with more than twenty years of experience handling countless family court cases across Southern California, I hear daily from parents determined to repair their relationships. Parents on both sides of custody arrangements face moments where choices either strengthen or weaken trust. For some, it's missed visits, anger-management mandates, or court-ordered steps left incomplete. For others, it's creating space for healing, honoring boundaries, or supporting consistent contact. Each misstep—whether by action or inaction—deepens hurt, erodes trust, and increases both legal and emotional barriers to reconnection.

These moments of disconnection—whether a missed visit, a broken boundary, or silence when words are needed—do not just appear in court records. They leave lasting gaps in the emotional fabric that binds families together.

Sometimes, I wish I could rewind time by just one minute to warn parents of the fallout. But that urgency is exactly why the family court system exists: to protect children, hold adults accountable, and offer a structured path back to safety and connection.

This workbook emerged from that understanding. You will not find quick fixes or compliance checklists here. Instead, you will discover a compassionate roadmap—an invitation to grow through accountability, rebuild trust with intention and care, and reclaim the connection you cherish.

Whether you are:

- A noncustodial parent striving to repair a fractured bond
- A custodial parent creating space for healing
- A specialist supporting families on this journey

This guide is crafted for you. You will confront past missteps, learn from them, and build a future founded on trust, resilience, and unity.

Facing the Perceptions of Bias

During intake sessions, I often hear fathers express that the family court system feels stacked against them. This perception is real and deserves acknowledgment. National data show that mothers are awarded primary custody in about 70–80% of cases, but most of these outcomes reflect caregiving history rather than explicit legal preference. When fathers actively seek custody, research indicates they succeed far more often than many expect—sometimes in nearly half of contested cases.

At the same time, it is important to recognize the mothers who find themselves in the noncustodial role. Though less common, their experiences carry a unique stigma and pain, as society often assumes mothers will always be the primary caregiver.

Whether father, mother, or guardian, every parent entering the family court system encounters unique challenges and perceptions of fairness. This workbook does not minimize those realities—it equips you to move forward despite them. It honors every parent's role, creating space for accountability, consistency, and reconnection.

By the Numbers: The Real Impact of Missed Reunification Steps

- **Court consequences are real.** Parents who repeatedly miss visits or fail to uphold agreements often face contempt actions, which may include fines, mandated make-up time, or even jail. Contempt is one of the most common enforcement tools used by family courts.

- **Consistency builds trust.** Research from the Child Welfare Information Gateway shows that families who maintain regular, court-ordered visits are significantly more likely to achieve timely reunification than those with sporadic compliance.
- **Children feel the strain.** National surveys (NSCH, HHS) show that children in foster care are 2–3 times more likely to experience anxiety, depression, or behavioral struggles compared to peers not in care—especially when reunification is prolonged or uncertain.
- **Custodial support matters.** Custodial parents who encourage consistent visitation and avoid unnecessary conflict significantly increase the likelihood of smoother reunification and reduced stress for children.

This workbook is not about blame—it is about building bridges. No matter your role, your choices matter, and your willingness to engage in this process is the first step toward healing.

HOW TO USE THIS WORKBOOK

Step 1: Orientation and Goal Setting

- Review the table of contents to see the overall flow.
- Outline your personal objectives:
- What do I hope to achieve through reunification?
- Which areas (communication, accountability, emotional healing) challenge me most? • Write these down as your baseline; your goals will evolve as you work through the workbook.

Step 2: Interactive Engagement

- Work through lessons in order, but revisit earlier sections as new insights arise.
- Complete every reflective question and journaling prompt.
- Maintain a dedicated journal alongside this workbook to capture your thoughts, emotions, and progress.

Step 3: Consolidate Learning into Action

- By lesson 10, integrate your insights into a customized Reconnection Plan with clear steps, timelines, and measurable goals.
- Prepare for ongoing growth by:
- Tracking progress in a simple log
- Celebrating milestones to keep motivation high

- Adapting strategies as your situation evolves
- Engage professional support when possible—periodic sessions with a therapist, coach, or trusted mentor can provide fresh perspectives and accountability.

Workbook Roadmap: Your Journey to Reconnection

This workbook is designed as a journey. Each part builds on the last, guiding you from reflection to action, and from action to lasting change. Here's what's ahead:

Part I – Foundations of Reconnection

Lessons 1–3: Understanding the cost of separation, why reconnection matters, and the principles of healing (hope, accountability, daily courage).

Part II – The Blueprint Framework

Lessons 4–7: Practical tools for preparing, building bridges, facing barriers,and creating daily acts of reconnection.

Part III – Tools for Families & Professionals

Lessons 8–10: Exercises for parents and children, guidance for therapists and advocates, and stories of hope.

Part IV – Sustaining the Journey

Lessons 11–13: Preventing relapse, creating a family vision, and passing healing forward as a legacy.

✨ Think of these four parts as stepping stones. Each one prepares you for the next, so by the time you reach Part IV, you're not just reconnecting—you're sustaining and passing on a legacy of healing. Now it is time to center yourself before your first **Assessment.**

PREPARING TO CHART YOUR COURSE

Before you begin the **Reunification Self-Assessment**, find a quiet space. Silence your phone and keep your journal or notebook ready.

Why This Matters

- It highlights your current strengths and blind spots.
- It turns abstract hopes into concrete insights you can track.
- It sets a clear baseline for measuring growth.
- How to Approach It
- Answer every question honestly and specifically.
- Note any prompt that feels vague and clarify it in writing.
- Release self-judgment—this is about awareness, not perfection.
- What to Do Next
- Complete each question without skipping.
- Tally your responses, then circle your highest and lowest scores.
- Use these insights to inform your first action step in Lesson 2.

When you are ready, begin your Reunification Self-Assessment. Let us chart your course together.

Reflection and Tracking

Building trust and accountability happens in the space between intention and action. Use the prompts, instructions, and table below as your guide. Fill in each cycle with your own details.

Reflection Prompts

- What went well in our conversation or activity?
- Which moments felt challenging or triggered frustration?
- How did I contribute to the positive outcomes?
- What could I have done differently to ease tension or misunderstanding?
- What new understanding do I carry forward into our next interaction?

Implementation Instructions

- Schedule a 10–15-minute check-in immediately after your session.
- Choose one reflection prompt and journal your answer in a dedicated notebook or digital file.
- Share insights with your counterpart (if appropriate) to model transparency.

- Define a SMART goal based on your reflection (Specific, Measurable, Achievable, Relevant, and Time-bound).

Tracking and Adjustment

- Each cycle, select one element to tweak. Common elements include:
- Communication style (tone, clarity, openness)
- Punctuality (arriving on time, meeting deadlines)
- Active listening (paraphrasing, asking follow-ups)
- Emotional tone (empathy, calmness, vulnerability)

Use the table below as your fill-in-the-blank tracker:

Cycle #	Date	Element	Goal	What Happened?
1	00/00/0000	Communication style	Speak with a calm, even tone in check-ins	Felt less defensive; partner opened more
2				
3				

Reunification Self-Assessment — Lesson 1

For each prompt:

- Rate yourself 1 (low) to 5 (high)
- Write your reflection or notes

1. What does "reconnection" mean to me, and what outcome do I hope to achieve?

Rate yourself (clarity of vision) 1–5: _____________

Reflection / Notes:

____

____

2. **How have my court-ordered violations shaped my family's emotional fabric?**

Rate yourself (insight into impact) 1–5: _____________

Reflection / Notes:

3. **Which behaviors created the deepest gaps in trust, and why?**

Rate yourself (understanding of trust gaps) 1–5: ___________

Reflection / Notes:

4. **What is my primary role and responsibility now as a parent committed to reconnection?**

Rate yourself (sense of responsibility) 1–5: ___________

Reflection / Notes:

5. **What emotions arise when I envision rebuilding my relationship, and how can they guide my next steps?**

Rate yourself (emotional awareness) 1–5: __

Reflection / Notes:

6. **What three concrete steps can I take today to begin mending gaps and fostering trust?**

Rate yourself (readiness for action) 1–5: ____________

Reflection / Notes:

____

____

Tally Your Scores Total Score__/ 30

Highest Score = current strength,
Lowest Score = priority area for focus

Charting the Course to Reconnection

In this opening lesson, you have mapped your personal Launchpad—defining what reconnection means for your family, confronting the emotional and legal fallout of past challenges, and spotlighting both your greatest strengths and the gaps that demand repair. By completing the **Reunification Self-Assessment**, you have:

- Clarified your vision for a renewed family bond
- Uncovered how past actions fractured trust and shaped dynamics
- Identified your core responsibilities and emotional landscape
- Committed to immediate, concrete steps that begin rebuilding trust

Hold on to these reflections and scores—they are the fuel for every strategy you will deploy in the lessons ahead.

Every parent, whether custodial or noncustodial, faces moments where choices either deepen the divide or begin to repair it. These moments are rarely comfortable, but they are always defining.

Next up is **Moment of Truth: When the fall becomes your launching pad**, where you will dive into the very fractures that cracked your family bonds. With unflinching honesty, you will transform those raw truths into the bedrock of your comeback.

This is not just a transition—it is the spark that ignites your transformation. Arm yourself with today's insights, steel your resolve, and press on: the real work—and the real change—begins now.

LESSON 2:
Recognizing Your Moment of Truth
When the fall becomes your launching pad

When silence answers where a promise should have been, this is the moment you either explain or begin to repair.

Title & Purpose

You walk into the house on a Saturday expecting the small, ordinary ritual that once anchored your week—a snack on the couch, a secret handshake, a story read aloud—and instead you find a silence that answers for you; a voicemail you never expected, a school photo turned sideways, a call that says *"they're upset."* In that silence lives the truth: a missed promise, a broken plan, a moment that names what's at stake.

After the incident comes the heat of feeling: a sudden, cold shame that sits behind the ribs; a rush of guilt that makes the simplest thought—"I *disappointed them*"—loop until you can't breathe; the flash of anger at yourself, at the system, at the clock that got in the way. There's an ache of longing that feels like hunger, a careful, desperate hope that wants to be believed when you say you'll do better. Too often those feelings push people into explanations or excuses, or into quiet resignation that this is the end of the story.

This is the **moment of truth**—when remorse is raw and the choice is simple but unforgiving: keep defending what happened, or convert that pain into a clear, visible set of actions that begin repair. Read Mark's case study next to see how one parent turned the ache of regret into the first steps of believable change.

Case Study:

Mark's Missed Visits

These are fictional composites created for educational purposes. Any resemblance to real persons is coincidental.

Background

Mark, balancing a demanding work schedule while struggling with alcohol dependency, began missing more than half of his scheduled weekend visits with his 8-year-old daughter, Emma.

What Went Wrong

- He failed to call ahead when running late
- He broke a promise to attend Emma's school play
- He refused court-offered supervised visits designed to rebuild trust.

Consequences

- The court reduced his parenting time to one supervised hour per month.
- Emma, feeling hurt and abandoned, stopped answering his calls.
- Mark sank into guilt so deep he considered giving up on reunification altogether.

Turning Point

Mark eventually recognized this as his *moment of truth*. With support, he entered intensive counseling, admitted his failures honestly to Emma's mother, and co-create a structured plan to prevent future breaches.

Lesson Learned

When a parent fails to meet commitments—whether court-ordered or relational—the fallout is two-fold:

- Legal: reduced visitation, fines, and contempt charges.
- Emotional: children feel abandoned, custodial parents feel betrayed, and the noncustodial parent may spiral into shame.

But these low points can also become launching pads. Honest accountability and a clear plan for change can transform a setback into the first step toward repair.

What It Entails

Missing or Late Visitations

Every no-show teaches your kids that promises do not matter. Even a five-minute delay without notice can sow confusion.

Ignoring Supervision or Safety Protocols

Skipping a supervised session isn't a small rebellion—it's a breakdown in agreed-upon safety your family counted on.

Failure to Communicate Changes or Emergencies

Not texting when you're stuck in traffic or failing to call when lost leaves everyone anxious and mistrustful.

Neglecting Financial Responsibilities

Falling behind on support payments or shared expenses isn't just a late check—it signals you're not investing in your child's present or future.

Any Breach of the Court-Ordered Plan

Whether it's skipping therapy, breaking curfews, or unauthorized overnight stays, each infraction chips away at your family's sense of security.

Why It Matters

Legal Fallout

- Reduced or modified visitation schedules that shrink your time with your kids
- • Fines or mandatory parenting courses that hit your wallet and pride
- Contempt proceedings that deepen conflict and drain court resources

Emotional Impact

- Children interpret absences as abandonment, internalizing guilt ("Maybe I'm not worth showing up for")
  - The custodial parent feels renewed betrayal, making future collaboration harder
  - You may spiral into shame and helplessness—but also stand at the threshold of transformation if you choose to step forward.

Key Statistics and Context

- **Visitation violations often lead to reduced or modified rights.** Family courts frequently respond to repeated missed visits or safety breaches by cutting back time or requiring supervision, prioritizing the child's stability.
- **Fines and parenting courses are common enforcement tools.** Judges regularly order financial penalties or mandatory classes to push parents toward accountability and skill-building.
- **Contempt charges remain a serious risk.** While less frequent than other sanctions, contempt proceedings can escalate quickly, leading to harsher restrictions or even jail time.

- **Children feel the impact deeply.** Research shows that children experiencing disrupted or inconsistent visitation are 2–3 times more likely to struggle with anxiety, withdrawal, or behavioral issues compared to peers in stable homes.
- **Custodial parents report high stress.** Studies confirm that ongoing visitation violations increase custodial parents' sense of betrayal and strain, making future collaboration harder.
- **Noncustodial parents often express regret.** Evaluations of fatherhood and reunification programs reveal that many parents acknowledge deep remorse after violations, and a significant portion eventually seek counseling or structured support.

⭐ Recognizing both the legal and emotional dimensions is step one toward transforming this low point into your personal launching pad for change.

Six-Step Recovery Process

You have confronted your moment of truth in all its legal and emotional force. This Six-Step Recovery Process turns that clarity into structured repair:

Step 1: Acknowledge the Violation

Goal: Own your breach so you rebuild from honesty, not excuses.

Actions:

- Stand before a mirror or journal and name each broken promise: "I missed our visit on X date…"
- Deliver a genuine apology—ideally in person—outlining what happened, why you regret it, and how you will do better
- Use "I" statements rather than deflecting blame

Step 2: Reflect on the Impact

Goal: See the human cost of your actions, not just the court's response.

Actions:

- Spend 10 minutes journaling how your child and co-parent experienced your absence
- • List specific examples: a missed birthday, a shift in your child's mood, questions they asked
- • If appropriate, invite your co-parent to share their perspective in writing or conversation

Step 3: Make Amends

Goal: Begin rebuilding trust through consistent, visible gestures.

Actions:

- Offer to add time to upcoming visits or participate in supervised support sessions
- • Draft a brief commitment plan: "For the next three visits, here's exactly when, where, and how I'll arrive."
- Follow up with a confirmation message 24 hours before each appointment

Step 4: Establish New Routines

Goal: Create predictability so your family can relax into certainty.

Actions:

- Set up a shared digital calendar with reminders for every hand-off
- Send a "Visit Confirmed" text 24 hours in advance and again one hour before • Build a simple ritual around each hand-off: a special handshake, a check-in question, or a brief family circle

Step 5: Seek Support and Resources

Goal: Layer personal effort with professional guidance and accountability.

Actions:

- Enroll in a court-approved parenting class, support group, or mediation session
- • Schedule bi-weekly check-ins with a therapist, coach, or mentor
- Identify an accountability partner who will remind you of commitments

Step 6: Monitor Progress and Adjust

Goal:

Keep momentum alive by reviewing wins, troubleshooting setbacks, and evolving your plan.

Actions:

- Host a monthly "Reconnection Review" to celebrate successes and surface challenges
- Track three key metrics—visit punctuality, communication check-ins, emotional-pulse surveys

- After each review, tweak one element: adjust reminder timings, refine your apology approach, or introduce a new ritual.

Next-Phase Transformation Roadmap

1. Craft a Unified Transformation Dashboard
2. Schedule Integrated Review and Feedback Sessions
3. Build Skills and Expand Your Support Network
4. Co-Create and Document a Relationship Blueprint
5. Embed Sustainable Self-Care Practices
6. Align Daily Habits with Your Vision
7. Embrace Iterative Growth

Why These Strategies

This roadmap bridges immediate repair and proactive reunification. By merging your metrics with narrative insights, scheduling regular reviews, expanding support, co-authoring clear protocols, embedding self-care, aligning daily habits, and embracing continuous feedback, you transform stop-gap fixes into a living, self-renewing family ecosystem.

Reflective Questions

1. **What core metrics and narrative insights will you include in your Transformation Dashboard, and how will they shape your focus?**

2. **Who will join your integrated review sessions, how often will you meet, and what agenda will you follow?**

3. **Which skills (e.g., conflict resolution, stress management) will you prioritize, and which workshops or peer resources will you engage?**

4. How will you co-create your Relationship Blueprint with your co-parent, and what non-negotiable norms and protocols will you define?

5. What sustainable self-care practices will you embed this week to maintain resilience, and how will you hold yourself accountable?

6. How will you solicit and integrate iterative feedback, and what cadence and process will ensure continuous roadmap evolution?

Conclusion

You have faced your lowest point head-on—naming every court-order breach, owning its legal and emotional fallout, and igniting the first sparks of accountability. These reflections are not about shame; they are the fuel for your comeback.

This moment of reckoning is not an endpoint but a Launchpad. Carry this momentum into **Lesson 3** — where you will forge iron-clad commitments, prove your reliability, and rebuild unshakable trust.

LESSON 3:
Step One
Accountability as the Gateway to Healing

Every journey of reconnection begins with a single, unshakable truth: **healing cannot happen without accountability.**

Accountability is not about punishment, shame, or endless self-criticism. It is about courage—the courage to face yourself honestly, to name what went wrong, and to choose actions that prove love is stronger than your excuses.

Think of accountability as the doorway you must walk through before trust can be rebuilt. You cannot skip it, and you cannot fake it. Children know when words are hollow. Co-parents know when promises are empty. Professionals know when effort is surface-level. But they also know when change is real—because accountability makes it visible.

This step is not glamorous. It is not easy. It asks you to sit with discomfort, to admit the harm caused, and to resist the urge to defend yourself. Yet it is also the most liberating step you will ever take. Why? Because once you own your story, no one else can use it against you. Ownership transforms regret into momentum.

In this lesson, you will learn how to turn remorse into responsibility, and responsibility into repair. You will see how one parent's willingness to face the truth became the turning point for his family. And you will be invited to begin your own process of accountability—one step at a time.

Real Story:

Jordan's Accountability Turnaround

These are fictional composites created for educational purposes. Any resemblance to real persons is coincidental.

Jordan had missed eight of twelve scheduled visits over three months, claiming "work chaos." When his daughter's voice messages turned from hopeful "Are we still on?" to anxious silence, he knew things had to change.

- **Step 1 (Awareness):** Jordan listed every missed visit in his journal and noted his daughter's growing anxiety and his co-parent's frustration.
- **Step 2 (Acknowledge Impact):** He sat down with his co-parent, owned each absence, and apologized sincerely for the worry he caused.
- **Step 3 (Commit to Change):** He pledged to confirm visits 48 hours ahead and, if he ever missed one, to write a two-page reflection and propose a make-up date within 24 hours.
- **Step 4 (Activate Support):** Jordan shared this Accountability Agreement with his co-parent and two close friends who agreed to weekly check-ins.
- **Step 5 (Reflect and Refine):** Tracking every confirmation and reflection in a shared dashboard, he hit 100 percent reliability the next month—and heard "See you Saturday!" instead of silence.

Jordan's story shows what accountability looks like in practice. Here is the **Five-Step Accountability Process**, broken down so you can apply it in your own journey.

The Essence of Accountability

Accountability is not punishment—it is clarity. It requires you to:

- Face the full reality of your actions
- Understand how those actions affected each family member
- Use that insight to guide consistent, positive change
- Realign your integrity and deepen connection by owning your story

What It Entails

- Owning every misstep with honesty: naming behaviors, dates, and contexts
- • Delivering apologies that acknowledge harm and express commitment
- • Mapping ripple effects on legal, emotional, and relational levels
- Drafting a written Accountability Agreement with clear actions and timelines
- Inviting mentors or peers to provide feedback and encouragement

Five-Step Accountability Process

Awareness

- Catalogue each breach in writing and note its legal/emotional impact.
- Share your journal with a trusted confidant to cement ownership.

Acknowledge Impact

- Hold a face-to-face conversation acknowledging exactly how your actions hurt others.
- Offer a genuine apology without excuses.

Commit to Change

- Draft an Accountability Agreement: define SMART actions, deadlines, and success metrics.
- Include specific "if-then" commitments (e.g., "If I miss a visit, then I will...").

Activate Support

- Share your Agreement with mentors, peers, or your co-parent.
- Schedule regular check-ins for feedback, encouragement, and corrective guidance.

Reflect and Refine

- Review your metrics and reflections monthly.
- Tweak one element each cycle to stay on track and deepen trust.

Why It Matters

- Rebuilds credibility faster than vague promises
- Deters future lapses through clear consequence awareness
- Honors your family's worth by showing up fully
- Creates momentum: each small win fuels confidence

Key Concepts of Accountability

Self-Recognition

Honest reflection pinpoints exactly where change is needed.

Understanding Impact

Clarifying legal, emotional, and relational consequences underscores urgency.

External Support

A network of mentors and peers sustains progress and provides perspective.

Key Statistics and Context

- **Writing down and sharing goals matters.** People who put their goals in writing and share them with a friend are 42% more likely to achieve them than those who don't (Dominican University of California study).
- **Parenting accountability agreements reduce repeat violations.** Family court and restorative justice research show that structured compliance plans help parents follow through more consistently and avoid repeated breaches.
- **Formal accountability structures improve co-parent collaboration.** Evidence from co-parenting programs demonstrates that structured interventions measurably reduce conflict and increase cooperation.
- **Accountability partners boost motivation.** Studies in recovery and behavioral change consistently find that individuals with a trusted accountability partner report higher motivation and lower relapse rates than those who go it alone.

✨ Accountability is not about punishment—it's about clarity, ownership, and building trust step by step.

Reflective Questions: Personalizing Your Accountability

1. Which specific behaviors or breaches will you list in the Awareness step, and how will you capture their unique impact?

2. How will you frame your apology and pledge in a way that resonates authentically with you and your co-parent?

3. What SMART actions will you define in your Accountability Plan to target your highest priority improvements?

4. Who will you choose as accountability partners, and what check-in frequency and format will fit your lifestyle?

5. Which metrics and data points will you track in your Transformation Dashboard, and how will you visualize them for clarity?

6. How will you run your monthly Monitor, Report and Adjust sessions to gather feedback and refine your plan?

Conclusion

Accountability as the Gateway to Healing

You have dug deep into your past, cataloguing each breach and feeling its full impact, then transformed remorse into a clear commitment. By moving through Awareness, Apologize and Pledge Change, Draft Your Accountability Plan, Engage Your Support Network, and Monitor, Report and Adjust, you did not just check boxes—you laid the foundation for genuine, lasting transformation.

This accountability framework is more than a lesson—it is the bedrock of your new path. Your reflective answers serve as both mirror and map, illuminating where you have been and guiding every decisive step ahead. Responsibility is not a finish line; it is an ongoing journey in which every honest admission, every kept promise, and every swift course correction rebuilds trust with your family—and with yourself.

With unshakable accountability now in place, you are poised to turn intention into predictable patterns of reliability. In the next lesson, you will explore proven strategies for the noncustodial parent to translate promises into consistent actions—rebuilding trust one dependable step at a time.

Part II
The Blueprint Framework

LESSON 4:
Consistency Builds Trust
The Power of Reliability

Title & Purpose

Reliability is the truest proof of change. In this lesson, you will move beyond isolated promises to weave consistency into every interaction with your children and co-parent. You will learn to establish rock-solid routines, transparent communication loops, and micro-commitments that accumulate into an unbroken track record of dependability. By the end, you will hold an actionable blueprint for turning good intentions into predictable presence—easing anxiety, earning confidence, and laying the foundation for genuine reconnection.

Case Study:

John's Journey to Rebuild Trust through Consistency

These are fictional composites created for educational purposes. Any resemblance to real persons is coincidental.

Background

John, a noncustodial parent, frequently arrived late or canceled visits at the last minute. His unpredictability left his children anxious and his co-parent on edge.

Turning Point

Realizing that sporadic effort would not repair the damage, John committed to shifting from chaos to consistency by designing clear routines and transparent communication loops.

Strategies Implemented

- **Establishing Routine:** Created a shared weekly calendar of visits, activities, and buffer times—synced across devices with automated reminders.
- **Transparent Communication:** Sent confirmation messages 24 hours before each visit and early notifications of unavoidable changes, offering alternatives.

- **Incremental Micro-Commitments:** Focused first on punctuality; each on-time arrival deposited small trust "credits."
- **Accountability Partners:** Enlisted a friend and a family counselor for weekly check-ins to review logs, troubleshoot obstacles, and celebrate wins.

Results and Impact

Within weeks, John achieved 100% on-time arrivals, his children greeted visits without anxiety, and his co-parent moved from skepticism to support. Family interactions became cooperative and joyful.

Key Statistics and Context

- **Accountability agreements reduce repeat violations.** Family court and restorative justice research show that structured compliance plans help parents follow through more consistently and avoid repeated breaches.
- **Shared scheduling and check-in tools improve collaboration.** Studies of co-parenting apps and structured communication protocols demonstrate measurable reductions in conflict and stronger cooperation between parents.
- **Accountability partners dramatically increase success.** Research shows that individuals with an accountability partner are up to 95% more likely to achieve their goals than those who rely on willpower alone.
- **Writing down and sharing commitments boosts follow-through.** People who record and share their goals are 42% more likely to achieve them than those who keep goals private.

✈ **Consistency isn't about perfection**—it's about building a track record of reliability that rewires trust over time.

What It Entails

Structured Scheduling Protocol

Draft a shared, device-synced calendar capturing every visit, event, and buffer. Automate reminders and grant co-parent access.

Transparent Check-In Rituals

Send concise pre- and post-visit confirmations in a group chat or family app. Log any changes with a brief rationale.

Incremental Micro-Commitments

Break "being reliable" into small promises—arrive ten minutes early, send midday reassurance texts, or propose make-up dates within 24 hours.

Dashboard Integration

Add consistency metrics (on-time rate, confirmation response time, follow-through percentage) to your Transformation Dashboard. Visualize streaks, spot anomalies, and celebrate milestones.

Accountability Partner Check-Ins

Recruit one or two trusted allies for weekly 15-minute syncs. They will call out lapses, brainstorm fixes, and reinforce progress.

Why It Matters

- **Reduces Anxiety and Builds Security**

Predictable routines and clear communication calm children's fears and ease co-parent concerns.

- **Provides Tangible Proof of Change**

Each kept micro-commitment becomes living evidence of your reliability.

- **Strengthens Co-Parent Collaboration**

Shared calendars and check-ins cut misunderstandings and conflict.

- **Creates Sustainable Trust Habits**

Over time, consistent actions shift from exception to norm, rewiring perceptions of your dependability.

- **Enables Real-Time Course Correction**

Dashboard metrics and partner check-ins surface issues immediately, turning potential setbacks into opportunities.

Six-Step Consistency Blueprint

Structured Scheduling Protocol

Draft and share a calendar of all visits, events, and buffer times, sync it across devices, automate reminders, and grant co-parent access.

1. **Transparent Check-In Rituals**

Confirm each visit 24 hours in advance and post a brief reflection afterward. Record any changes with a one-line reason.

2. **Incremental Micro-Commitments**

Choose one small promise (e.g., arrive 10 minutes early). Focus on it for a week until it sticks, then layer on the next.

3. **Dashboard Integration**

Track key metrics—punctuality rate, confirmation response time, follow-through percentage—on your dashboard. Flag dips below targets.

4. **Accountability Partner Check-Ins**

Enlist allies for weekly syncs. Review your scheduling log, share dashboard data, and invite candid feedback.

5. **Ongoing Review and Adaptation**

Monthly, audit performance: compare metrics to targets, pinpoint shortfalls, adjust buffers or reminders, set the next micro-commitment, and archive the report.

The Consistency Blueprint starts by mapping out a shared, synced schedule with built-in buffers and automated reminders, then layering in clear pre- and post-visit confirmations logged in a family chat or app. You will zero in on one small reliability promise each week—like arriving early— while monitoring your on-time rate, confirmation response time, and follow-through percentage on a central dashboard. Weekly check-ins with accountability partners keep you honest and motivated, and a monthly review lets you celebrate successes, troubleshoot setbacks, tweak reminders or buffers, and choose your next micro-commitment. This cycle turns isolated efforts into an unbroken record of dependable presence.

Reflective Questions

1. How will you design and share your scheduling protocol to cover every visit, event, and buffer time?

2. What will your check-in rituals look like—timing, channels, and content—and how will you document them?

3. Which micro-commitment will you focus on this week, and what specific actions will it involve?

4. Which consistency metrics will you track on your dashboard, and how will you visualize them to catch trends?

5. Who will serve as your accountability partner(s), and what will your weekly check-in process entail?

6. How will you run your ongoing review each month to refine your protocols and set the next micro-commitment?

Conclusion

You have transformed ad-hoc assurances into a steady heartbeat of reliability—every shared calendar update, confirmation message, micro-commitment, dashboard metric, partner check in, and monthly tweak proving your change in real time. That consistency now speaks louder than words, soothing anxiety and earning your family's genuine confidence.

With reliability firmly in place, it is time to build partnership. Lesson 5 turns to the custodial parent's role in co-creating reconnection—exploring how mutual support, open dialogue, and shared rituals magnify your consistent efforts and propel the healing journey forward.

LESSON 5:
The Custodial Parent's Role

Supporting the Reconnection Journey

Title & Purpose

As the custodial parent, your choices can either build bridges of trust or sow the seeds of parental alienation. In this lesson, you will move beyond gatekeeping to become an active partner— reinforcing the noncustodial parent's consistent efforts while shielding your children from any divisive messages. You will co-design communication rituals that prevent subtle alienating behaviors, establish clear feedback loops to keep both parents aligned, and embed predictable routines that let reliability shine through. By the end, you will hold a concrete blueprint for creating a stable, emotionally safe environment where trust—not suspicion—takes root.

Overview

In Lesson 4, the noncustodial parent laid the groundwork for unwavering reliability through structured routines, transparent check-ins, micro-commitments, and accountability systems. Now your active collaboration multiplies those solo efforts into a cohesive, trust-building journey. Studies show that children with unpredictable visitation schedules are significantly more likely to experience heightened anxiety and behavioral issues—underscoring why your role as gatekeeper or partner matters more than ever.

Case Study:

Maria's Co-Parenting Collaboration

These are fictional composites created for educational purposes. Any resemblance to real persons is coincidental.

Background

Maria was wary when her ex-spouse, David, missed visits and left their daughter feeling anxious. She worried that stepping back would seem like approval of his past unreliability.

Turning Point

After Lesson 4 coaching, Maria chose partnership over protection. She invited David into a weekly scheduling ritual, framing each interaction as a shared commitment to their daughter's well-being.

Strategies Implemented

- **Collaborative Scheduling**: Maria created a shared calendar on their phones, blocking visit windows, activities, and buffer times.
- **Open Feedback Loop**: She sent a brief "How did it go?" message after each visit and encouraged David to do the same.
- **Positive Framing**: Maria praised punctual arrivals publicly ("Sofia lit up when you showed on time!") and validated disappointment if he slipped.
- **Joint Accountability**: They invited their family counselor into weekly 10-minute check-ins to troubleshoot hiccups and celebrate milestones.

Results and Impact

Within two months, David's reliability improved dramatically. Their daughter's nightly journal entries shifted from "I miss him" to "I love our Saturdays," and Maria found herself trusting David's commitments—and modeling that trust to their child.

What It Entails

Structured Scheduling Protocol

Draft a shared, device-synced calendar capturing every visit, event, and buffer. Automate at least two reminders and grant co-parent edit access to eliminate uncertainty.

Transparent Check-In Rituals

Send concise pre- and post-visit confirmations in a dedicated family chat. Log any changes immediately, noting the reasons and proposed alternatives.

Collaborative Expectation-Setting

Co-author a simple "Visitation Pact" outlining arrival windows, communication timeframes, and make-up visit options to ensure both parents honor the same standards.

Dashboard Integration

Research on co-parenting apps and structured scheduling shows that families who adopt these tools experience significantly fewer conflicts and missed visits.

Accountability Partner Check-Ins

Recruit one or two trusted allies (friend, coach, and counselor) to review your joint calendar and dashboard weekly. They spotlight lapses, brainstorm fixes, and reinforce progress together.

Ongoing Review and Adaptation

At month's end, audit successes and shortfalls. Adjust buffer times, refine communication templates, and set a new micro-commitment focus. Archive each report as a milestone in your co-parenting journey.

Why It Matters

Reduces Parental Alienation

Your active partnership blocks subtle excluding behaviors, keeping both parents equally present in your children's minds.

Builds Emotional Security

Predictable routines and open feedback calm children's fears, lowering the anxiety that often rises when schedules are erratic or inconsistent.

Strengthens Co-Parent Collaboration

Shared expectations and transparent communication consistently reduce misunderstandings and conflict, creating smoother interactions.

Models Healthy Relationship Skills

Demonstrating cooperation and mutual respect teaches your children how to navigate differences constructively.

Accelerates Reconnection

When both parents align on reliability standards, trust grows faster— transforming solo efforts into a unified healing journey.

Key Takeaways immediately

- Shared, synced calendars with reminders create clear expectations and reduce uncertainty.
- Real-time check-ins and change logs foster transparent collaboration and prevent misunderstandings.
- A mutual "Visitation Pact" aligns both parents on standards, making routines predictable and fair.
- Tracking progress with a shared dashboard provides measurable proof of reliability and highlights growth.
- Weekly ally check-ins with a counselor, coach, or trusted friend sustain accountability and encouragement.
- Monthly reviews and adjustments ensure continuous improvement, turning small wins into lasting trust.

Consistency and collaboration are the custodial parent's most powerful tools for transforming reliability into reconnection.

Reflective Questions

1. **How will you design and share your structured scheduling protocol to cover every visit, event, and buffer time?**

2. **What will your transparent check-in rituals involve—timing, channels, and documentation—and how will you log each change?**

3. **How will you co-author a "Visitation Pact" with your co-parent, and what mutual standards will it establish?**

4. **Which dashboard metrics will you track (on-time rate, response times, and follow-through) and how will you visualize trends?**

5. Who will serve as your accountability partner(s), and what will your weekly check-in process include?

6. How will you structure your monthly review and adaptation sessions to refine your co-parenting blueprint and set the next focus?

Conclusion

You have shifted from solitary gatekeeping to a vibrant partnership that transforms reliability into reconnection. By co-creating a shared scheduling protocol, enshrining transparent check-in rituals, drafting a mutual Visitation Pact, and weaving real-time metrics with accountability partners, you have built more than punctual visits—you have built a sanctuary of trust. Every confirmation message and weekly audit now serves as tangible proof that two aligned parents can banish alienation, soothe their children's anxieties, and model cooperative respect. This dynamic collaboration does not simply maintain a calendar of commitments; it reshapes your family's narrative. Where uncertainty once reigned, you have planted the seeds of security and mutual responsibility. You have shown your children that both parents can honor their word, creating a home environment where openness, shared decision-making, and consistency are the new normal.

Carry forward this momentum as you prepare to delve even deeper into your children's experiences. Lesson 5's blueprint has given you the tools to rebuild trust together—now it is time to understand the emotional world you have helped stabilize.

Transition into Lesson 6: Children's Inner Worlds Understanding Emotional Impact

In Lesson 6, you will turn your focus to what lies beneath each smile or tear. You will learn to recognize subtle emotional cues, validate your children's feelings without judgment, and adapt your co-parenting strategies to meet their evolving inner needs. By exploring children's inner worlds, you will gain the insight needed to nurture their resilience, deepen your emotional connection, and ensure that every structural routine and transparent ritual supports not just reliability, but genuine emotional healing.

LESSON 6:
The Children's Inner World
Understanding Emotional Impact

Title & Purpose

Your child is not just along for the ride—they feel every schedule change, check-in, and promise in vivid emotional color. In this lesson, you will step into their shoes: anticipate waves of anxiety, relief, hope, and even guilt tied to each visitation, and respond with precise support. By the end, you will have a toolbox of proven strategies for decoding their signals, co-regulating overwhelming feelings, and creating an emotional safety net that accelerates healing and solidifies trust.

Overview

With structured routines and transparent communication in place, your child enjoys predictability. Now it is time to pair reliability with deep emotional attunement. We begin by mapping the emotional journey your child experiences before, during, and after visits so you can meet them exactly where they are and guide them toward resilience.

Case Study:

7-Year-Old Ella's Emotional Journey

These are fictional composites created for educational purposes. Any resemblance to real persons is coincidental.

Ella began showing stomachaches and school avoidance the day before her dad's visits, then retreated into silence afterwards. Her "worry scale" entries averaged 8/10.

Applying Lesson 6:

Ella's parents mapped her emotional phases and started a simple emotion journal.

They instituted a two-minute breathing ritual before every handoff and provided a comfort object she could carry between homes.

Open-ended check-ins ("What made you laugh today?") replaced "How was your visit?"

Within five weeks, Ella's worry scores dropped significantly, her somatic complaints subsided, and she began sharing both highs and lows freely in their nightly storytelling circle.

Mapping the Emotional Phases

Children typically move through five phases tied to visits:

Anticipatory Anxiety

Restlessness, sleep disturbances, or clinginess as they brace for change.

Pre-Visit Excitement

A hopeful mood spike tinged with fear it could all fall through.

Visit Immersion

Joy mixed with guilt and hyper-vigilance about time.

Post-Visit Transition

Tears, withdrawal, or irritability reconciling happy memories with separation.

Resettling Phase

Gradual calm—unless a cancellation re-ignites anxiety and sends them back up the curve.

Recognizing these phases arms you to pre-empt distress, validate their experience, and smooth each transition.

Decoding Behavioral and Verbal Cues

Watch for subtler signs beyond tears:

Behavioral Signals

Regression (bed-wetting, thumb-sucking), school avoidance, sudden clinginess, or outbursts of anger.

Verbal Clues

"I don't want to go," offhand comments like "He doesn't love me," or vague complaints of tummy aches.

Physical Indicators

Headaches, appetite changes, or fatigue—often somatic expressions of emotional distress.

Action Steps:

Keep an emotion journal noting dates, behaviors, and triggers. Compare patterns against your visitation calendar. Share observations with your co-parent and, if needed, a child therapist.

Co-Regulation Techniques

When their emotions surge, your calm presence is the anchor:

Calming Rituals

Practice deep breathing together— "smell the flower, blow out the candle"—for two minutes before transitions.

Safe Touch

A hand on the shoulder, a gentle back rub, or a warm hug signals security.

Emotion Check-Ins

Use a simple chart (happy, sad, mad, and worried) and ask: "What's your color right now?" Name, do not numb.

Grounding Exercises

Try a "5-4-3-2-1" sense walk: identify 5 things you see, 4 you hear, and so on to refocus on the present.

Consistent co-regulation teaches self-soothing skills and builds trust in your support.

Empathetic Conversation Framework

Move beyond "How was your visit?" with validating dialogue:

Open-Ended Questions

"Tell me about the best moment today," or "What felt hard when you were there?"

Reflective Listening

Mirror their words: "It sounds like you felt worried when plans changed."

Narrative Scaffolding

Help them build a coherent story: "When visits shift, it is normal to feel upset. Next time, you might...."

Emotion Labeling

Name the feeling: "That sounds like disappointment. Let us figure out what you need." Modeling empathy empowers emotional growth and deepens your connection.

Creating an Emotional Safety Net

Design outlets that signal, "It's safe to share":

Storytelling Circles

Weekly check-ins where each person shares a highlight and a challenge—just listening.

Mood Journals

Provide art supplies or a notebook for doodles, stories, or sentences about feelings.

Worry Boxes

A decorated container where your child drops written or drawn worries; open and discuss one daily.

Comfort Objects

A stuffed animal or blanket that travels between homes, carrying a familiar scent. These rituals anchor predictability and remind your child that their inner world matters.

Age-Specific Considerations

Tailor your approach to developmental stage:

- **Littles (3–6)** Use play, drawings, and storybooks to surface emotions.
- **Elementary (7–10)** Introduce mood journals and "color" check-ins.
- **Tweens and Teens (11–17)** Ask about physical sensations ("Where do you feel that?") and consider private digital check-ins.

Key Takeaways immediately

- Anticipate and normalize anxiety spikes.
- Spot behavioral, verbal, and physical cues.
- Anchor with co-regulation rituals.
- Deepen connection through empathetic dialogue.
- Bolster safety with storytelling, journals, worry boxes, and comfort objects.

Why It Matters

- Reduces anxiety and behavioral flare-ups by anchoring your child in relational safety.
- Prevents mislabeling emotional distress as misbehavior.
- Strengthens the parent-child bond, accelerating trust rebuilt through reliability.

Reflective Questions

1. Which emotional phase does your child struggle with most, and how will you prepare them?

2. What specific cues (behavioral, verbal, physical) have you noticed, and how will you journal them?

3. Which co-regulation technique will you practice consistently over the next week?

Conclusion

You have moved beyond mere reliability to become deeply attuned to your child's emotional world—anticipating their fears, decoding their cues, and co-regulating their big feelings. The rituals, conversations, and safety nets you have established in Lesson 6 do not just smooth transitions; they send a powerful message that your child's inner life matters and that both parents stand ready to support them.

In Lesson 7, we will turn our focus to the words and tones that shape your co-parenting relationship. You will learn to build conversational bridges that validate emotions, de-escalate conflicts, and align both parents around a shared vision for your family's healing. Together, we will explore:

- Techniques for listening that invite openness rather than defensiveness
- Phrasing strategies that honor each parent's intentions without blame
- Feedback loops that keep dialogue constructive and solution-focused

With these communication bridges in place, you will ensure that every interaction—whether with your co-parent or your child—becomes an opportunity to heal, connect, and reinforce the trust you have worked so hard to rebuild.

LESSON 7:
Communication Bridges
Speaking to Heal, Not to Win

Title & Purpose

Your words can build bridges or walls. In this lesson, you will learn to shift from winning arguments to fostering healing by using communication strategies that validate emotions, de-escalate conflict, and align co-parents around shared goals. You will practice active listening, "I" statements, and structured feedback loops to speak in ways that invite cooperation and reinforce trust.

Overview

With reliability and emotional attunement established, the final piece is how you talk—to each other and to your child. Misguided words can trigger defensiveness or alienation, undermining all you have built. In this lesson, you will explore communication frameworks that turn conversations into collaborative problem-solving sessions, transforming potential flashpoints into opportunities for deeper connection and joint growth.

Case Study:

Sam and Leah's Shift from Conflict to Collaboration

These are fictional composites created for educational purposes. Any resemblance to real persons is coincidental.

Background

Sam and Leah splintered into heated text threads over missed pickups and scheduling changes. Their messages flared with blame: "You're always late" and "You don't care about my time."

Turning Point

After Lesson 6, they recognized how tone and framing fueled resentment. They agreed to restructure their communication using Healing Language principles.

Strategies Implemented

- Active Listening: In weekly 15-minute calls, they paraphrased each other's concerns before responding.
- I-Statements: They replaced "You never" with "I feel worried when pickup times change."
- Scheduled Feedback Rituals: They set a "No-Blame Friday" check-in with a clear agenda. • Collaborative Problem-Solving: Each conversation ended with "What can we try next time?" and documented agreed actions.

Results and Impact

Within a month, arguments dropped noticeably. Text threads became shorter and calmer, and pickups ran smoothly. Their child noticed the difference and said, "It's nice when you two talk like a team."

Key Communication Frameworks and What It Entails

Active Listening

What it entails:

- Give your full attention—no multitasking.
- Mirror back key points: "What I am hearing is... Is that right?"
- Ask clarifying questions before responding.
- I-Statements and Nonviolent Communication

What it entails:

- Structure each message as "I feel [emotion] when [situation], because [need].
- Would you be willing to [request]?"
- Replace "You always..." with "I feel..." to own emotions and reduce defensiveness.
- End with a clear, actionable request.

Repair Language

What it entails:

- Acknowledge missteps immediately: "I'm sorry I..."
- Explain the emotion behind your reaction: "...because I was upset."
- Propose an amendment: "Next time, I'll...."

Constructive Feedback Loops

What it entails:

- Schedule regular check-ins with a defined agenda.
- Start with positives, then address concerns, and end with joint solutions.
- Document agreed actions in a shared note or calendar.
- Reframing Criticism into Collaboration

What it entails:

- Swap "You did this wrong" for "Let's figure out how to avoid this next time."
- Use "we" language: "How can we make this work better?"
- Focus on solutions, not faults.
- Positive Check-In Rituals

What it entails:

- Send a daily gratitude text: "Today I appreciated you when…"
- Hold a weekly appreciation round: each parent names one thing they valued about the other.
- Keep these exchanges brief, specific, and genuine.

Why It Matters

- Decreases conflict-driven stress and structured communication strategies significantly reduce the frequency and intensity of heated exchanges.
- • Models healthy conflict resolution for your child.
- Keeps focus on shared goals—your child's well-being—rather than blame.
- Transforms missteps into learning moments, reinforcing growth over guilt.

Key Takeaways briefly

- Listen first, speak second: understanding builds trust.
- "I" statements clarify needs and reduce defensiveness.
- Repair language stops small rifts from widening.
- Scheduled feedback turns conflict into collaboration.
- Reframing fosters joint problem-solving.
- Positive check-ins sustain goodwill and mutual appreciation.

Reflective Questions

1. How will you structure your next active listening session to ensure both parents feel heard?

2. What "I" statement will you craft to address a recent tension without blame?

3. How can you ritualize language repair when a conversation heats up?

4. Which feedback ritual format (time, agenda, medium) will you adopt and why?

5. How will you reframe a past critique into a collaborative request?

6. What positive check-in ritual will you start this week to reinforce mutual appreciation?

Conclusion

You have turned potential battlegrounds into bridges of healing—using active listening, "I" statements, repair language, and structured feedback to validate emotions, de-escalate conflict, and align co-parents around your child's well-being. Every conversation now reinforces trust rather than erodes it, modeling healthy conflict resolution for your children and solidifying the foundation you built through reliability and emotional attunement.

Carry forward this newfound communication climate. The collaborative spirit you have fostered will not just ease tensions between you and your co-parent; it will also create a calm, supportive backdrop for the next phase of your family's journey.

Transition into Lesson 8: Bonding Anew

Reconnecting with the Children

With communication bridges in place, it is time to focus on direct bonding with your kids. In Lesson 8, you will explore creative rituals, play-based interactions, and meaningful experiences designed to deepen emotional ties and celebrate the progress you have made. These intentional bonding practices will harness your strong co-parenting collaboration and transform it into joyful, lasting connections with your children.

Part III
Tools for Family & Professionals

LESSON 8: Bonding Anew
Reconnecting with the Children

Title & Purpose

Effective reunification is not complete until the emotional bridge between you and your child is fully restored. In this lesson, you will learn a six-step process to rebuild trust, spark genuine joy, and revive the sense of safety your child requires. Drawing on attachment science and creative engagement techniques, you will move beyond logistics into moments of true presence and belonging. By the end, you will possess a toolkit of practical strategies that transform every interaction into an opportunity for deep reconnection.

Overview and Story Hook

These are fictional composites created for educational purposes. Any resemblance to real persons is coincidental.

Six-year-old Zoe felt untethered after weeks of switching homes. Her laughter faded, questions grew quiet, and she clung to every drop-off. One evening, Mom set aside her phone and knelt beside Zoe. With a soft voice, she asked, "What part of today felt lonely?" Zoe's big eyes welled up. Then Mom said, "I am here to listen. Would you draw me your favorite spot on the playground?" As Zoe sketched bright swings and her best friend's face, her tension melted—and her laughter returned. That simple act of undivided attention and co-creation reminded Zoe that her feelings matter and that her bond with her parents is unbreakable.

What It Entails and Six-Step Reconnect Process

Step 1: Create Emotional Safety

- **Technique:** Drop distractions – phones, schedules, tasks – and adopt open body language. Kneel or sit beside your child, make eye contact, and say, "I'm here, and your feelings are safe with me."
- **Drill:** Practice this posture and phrase three times today in quiet moments.
- **Impact:** Your child learns any emotion they share will be met with acceptance.

Step 2: Launch Open-Ended Check-Ins

- **Technique:** Replace "How was your day?" with prompts like "What surprised you today?" or "What felt hard?" Then sit in silence—let your child fill the space.
- **Drill:** Write five open-ended questions on cards; draw one at dinner each night.
- **Impact:** These questions uncover genuine stories and hidden emotions.

Step 3: Practice Affirmation and Validation

- **Technique:** Reflect their emotion and celebrate their strength. For example, "You felt disappointed when playtime ended, and I admire how patiently you asked for five more minutes."
- **Drill:** After each check-in, name one feeling you heard and one quality you admire.
- **Impact:** Validation teaches your child that their feelings matter and that they have inner resources to draw on.

Step 4: Co-Create New Rituals

- **Technique:** Invite your child to design a weekly bonding ritual—a "Memory Jar" for notes of gratitude or a Saturday "Adventure Hour" park exploration.
- **Drill:** Brainstorm three ritual ideas together; pick one to start this week.
- **Impact:** Ownership of the ritual boosts engagement and creates shared anticipation.

Step 5: Use Play and Creativity

- **Technique:** Leverage art, games, or storytelling to open emotional doors. Build a "Feelings Wheel" from paper and markers—spin and share a memory matching the color.
- **Drill:** Choose one creative activity to do together before the weekend.
- **Impact:** Play dissolves barriers, letting children express themselves without pressure.

Step 6: Reflect and Grow Together

- **Technique:** Schedule a weekly "Connection Check"—just five minutes to discuss what brought you closer and what could feel more supportive. Record insights in a shared notebook.
- **Drill:** Set a recurring calendar reminder for your Connection Check.

- **Impact:** Regular reflection turns breakthroughs into a living, evolving partnership.

Why It Matters

- Strengthens attachment: Secure bonds are consistently linked to fewer behavior challenges and greater cooperation.
- Builds resilience: Children who feel heard learn to navigate emotions with confidence.
- Models' healthy connection: Your presence teaches empathy, curiosity, and trust.
- Transforms routines into rituals: Small, consistent actions become lasting sources of security.

Key Statistics

- Regular connection rituals (like weekly five-minute check-ins) strengthen emotional closeness and reduce loneliness, according to national surveys and health advisories.
- Open-ended check-ins uncover hidden emotions and are linked to lower stress and stronger resilience in both children and adults.
- Family rituals (shared meals, traditions, or co-created promises) consistently predict better child adjustment, reduced conflict spillover, and stronger family bonds.
- Creative play fosters emotional expression, empathy, and social-emotional growth, helping children share difficult feelings more freely.
- Daily affirmations and positive reflection exercises support anger management and reduce emotional outbursts.
- Intentional listening practices (active, empathetic attention) improve emotional regulation and model healthy communication skills.

Age-Specific Adaptations

- **Littles (3–5):** Use puppets or stuffed animals to role-play emotions. Keep questions to two choices (e.g., "Happy or worried?").
- **Elementary (6–9):** Introduce mood journals with simple drawings and one-word check-ins.
- **Tweens (10–13):** Invite text-based check-ins if they prefer privacy; ask about physical sensations ("Where do you feel that in your body?").

- **Teens (14–17):** Offer choice—face-to-face, voice note, or chat. Empower them to co-design rituals and set the agenda.

Key Takeaways

- Emotional safety is the bedrock of reconnection.
- Open-ended prompts reveal what lies beneath.
- Affirmation and validation fuel self-esteem.
- Rituals co-created with your child deepen engagement.
- Play invites authentic expression.
- Reflection cements progress and sparks growth.

Reflective Questions

1. **Which step in the reconnect process will you focus on first, and how will you practice it this week?**

2. **What new weekly ritual will you co-design, and how will you involve your child in planning?**

3. **How will you adapt these techniques to your child's developmental stage? Give one concrete example.**

4. **How will you use play and creativity to open emotional doors—and which activity will you schedule this week?**

5. **What does your ideal weekly "Connection Check" look like—and how will you capture insights to guide your next bonding drill?**

6. **Which two affirmation-and-validation phrases will you practice daily to reinforce your child's strengths—and when will you intentionally deliver them?**

Conclusion

You have journeyed from checking the calendar to checking in with the heart. Through our six-step Reconnect Process, you have learned how to:

- Establish emotional safety by dropping distractions and opening a space where any feeling is welcome.
- Ask questions that uncover your child's hidden hopes and fears, giving them language for what they experience.
- Validate their emotions and celebrate their strengths so they know they are seen and supported.
- Co-create rituals that your child eagerly anticipates, turning ordinary moments into shared memories.
- Use play and creativity to dissolve barriers, letting authentic connection flow naturally.
- Reflect together each week, cementing breakthroughs and guiding your next step in real time.

These tools have done more than smooth transitions—they have reignited joy, rebuilt trust, and anchored your child in the certainty of your presence. You have transformed routines into heartfelt rituals and logistical handoffs into moments of belonging. Every drawn "Memory Jar" note, every spun "Feelings Wheel," and every five-minute Connection Check has woven a stronger emotional bond, laying the groundwork for lasting security.

Carry this momentum forward by treating every interaction as an invitation: a chance to listen more deeply, to play more freely, and to celebrate the small wins that signal your child's growing confidence. Your consistent presence and intentional rituals will ripple through their world, teaching them that relationships are not just reliable—they are joyous, evolving, and built on mutual trust.

With your emotional reconnection toolkit now in hand, the next step is uniting your co-parenting approach into a seamless partnership. In Lesson 9, **Co-Parenting in Practice,** we will explore how to:

- Integrate your scheduling protocols, emotional attunement, and healing communication into everyday routines.
- Align expectations and responsibilities with your co-parent to present a united front.
- Troubleshoot real-world challenges—school events, holidays, unexpected conflicts— together.
- Embed celebration ceremonies and growth milestones so your practices become second nature.

By the end of the next lesson, you will not just practice co-parenting; you will embody it—creating a cohesive, supportive environment that nurtures your child's well-being and cements the foundation you have worked so hard to rebuild.

LESSON 9:
Co-Parenting in Practice
Aligning for Family Restoration

Title & Purpose

You have built the pillars—reliability, emotional attunement, healing communication, and bonding rituals. Now it is time to fuse them into a single, unstoppable force. In this lesson, you will co-create your Family Restoration Blueprint, a living plan that aligns every schedule, conversation, and ritual around your child's thriving. By the end, you will launch daily, weekly, and monthly practices that turn your co-parenting strategies into seamless, joy-powered action.

Overview and Story Hook

These are fictional composites created for educational purposes. Any resemblance to real persons is coincidental.

The Nguyen family had mastered the rituals of Lesson 8, yet Friday ended in mixed messages and a tense handoff. One evening, they sat side by side—Mom with her tablet and Dad with his planner—and sketched a unified "Family Restoration Blueprint" on a giant calendar wall. In that moment, the disjointed tactics snapped into alignment, transforming stress into synergy. By month's end, their daughter's bedtime journal overflowed with "I feel safe" and "I can't wait for tomorrow."

What It Entails and Alignment Blueprint

Map and Merge Your Ecosystem

- **Technique:** Gather every calendar, app, and ritual into one shared hub.
- **Drill:** Host a 30-minute "Blueprint Workshop" with sticky notes listing routines, check-ins, and rituals. Group by timing and purpose.
- **Impact:** Full visibility eliminates double-books and hidden agendas.

Launch the Daily "Three-Point Huddle"

- **Technique:** Each morning, answer three prompts: "Today's must-wins," "Potential hiccups," and "Emotional check-in for [Child Name]."

- **Drill:** Keep it to 3 minutes and log in a shared note.
- **Impact:** Small alignment defuses surprises and unites you around daily goals.

Fire-Drill Conflict Response

- **Technique:** Apply the 3-Step Recenter when friction flares:
  Breathe and ground
  Name the shared goal ("We both want Emma to feel safe")
  Propose one next step
- **Drill:** Practice during a low-stakes rehearsal.
- **Impact:** Prevents flashpoints from derailing your Blueprint.

Hold a Weekly "Lab Session"

- **Technique:** Block 20 minutes to review metrics (on-time rate, check-in consistency, emotional pulse), celebrate wins, and adjust one micro-commitment.
- **Drill:** Use your shared dashboard to spotlight a 10% improvement goal each week. •
- **Impact:** Continuous refinement turns progress into momentum.

Create a Celebration and Milestone Calendar

- **Technique:** Schedule monthly "Family Festivals" (picnics, game nights) and quarterly "Growth Ceremonies" to highlight milestones.
- **Drill:** Draft this calendar at your next Blueprint Workshop and set automated invites.
- **Impact:** Ritualized celebrations reinforce every step of reconnection.

Build a Shared Growth Dashboard

- **Technique:** Consolidate KPIs from Lessons 4–8—visit punctuality, emotional check-in scores, and conflict-free exchanges— into one visual board.
- **Drill:** Co-design your dashboard's layout; choose 3–5 metrics to track publicly.
- **Impact:** Data-driven clarity keeps motivation high and accountability shared.

Monthly Reflection and Recharge Retreat

- **Technique:** Treat yourselves to a 1-hour co-parent retreat—coffee, waffles, and guided prompts: "What legacy do we want to leave?" "Which connection sparks felt electric this month?"
- **Drill:** Block this on your calendar three months in advance.

- **Impact:** Intentional pause fuels next-level commitment and creativity.

Age-Specific Adaptations

- **Littles (3–5):** Use drawings and stickers in your Blueprint Workshop. Shorten huddles to one prompt (e.g., "Today's happy moment").
- **Elementary (6–9):** Incorporate a simple sticker chart on the Growth Dashboard. Let them pick one goal each week.
- **Tweens (10–13):** Invite them to co-host the Weekly Lab Session and contribute to metric selection.
- **Teens (14–17):** Offer choice of digital huddles (voice note, text) and let them lead the Monthly Retreat's agenda.

Common Pitfalls and Course-Corrections

- **Stale Dashboard:** Schedule a "Dashboard Detox" to streamline tracking and remove outdated KPIs.
- **Workshop Fatigue:** Rotate facilitators between parents and keep sticky-note sessions under 30 minutes.
- **Tech Overload:** Alternate digital and analog tools—paper wall calendars one month, shared apps the next.
- **Skipped Retreats:** Automate invites and tether retreats to enjoyable outings (coffee shop, park).

Tools and Resources

- Shared Calendars: Google Calendar with co-parent access
- Collaboration Apps: Trello or Miro for your Blueprint Workshop
- Dashboard Platforms: Google Sheets, Notion, or a dedicated co-parenting app
- Reflection Prompts: Downloadable PDF of Monthly Retreat questions
- Printable Blueprint Canvas (see Appendix)

Next-Steps Checklist

☐ Schedule your first 30-minute Blueprint Workshop this week

☐ Set up the Daily Three-Point Huddle reminder

☐ Define and display your 3–5 Shared Growth Dashboard metrics

☐ Plan your first Family Festival and automate calendar invites

☐ Block out your upcoming Monthly Reflection and Recharge Retreat

☐ Review and streamline your tools: pick one calendar and one dashboard app

Appendix: Family Restoration Blueprint Canva

Key Takeaways at a Glance

Step	Activity	Schedule	Owner
Map and Merge Your Ecosystem	Sticky-note Workshop	Week 1	Both
Daily Three-Point Huddle	Morning Alignment check	Daily check (3 min)	Both
Fire-Drill Conflict Response	3-Step Recenter drill	As needed	Both
Weekly Lab Session	Metrics review and micro-commitment	Weekly (20 min)	Both
Celebration and Milestone Calendar	Family Festival and Growth Ceremony	Monthly/Quarterly	Both
Shared Growth Dashboard	Metric tracking board	Ongoing	Both
Reflection and Recharge Retreat	Co-parent guided retreat	Monthly	Both

- A unified Blueprint transforms scattered tactics into a cohesive strategy.
- Micro-huddles and lab sessions forge daily and weekly alignment.
- Fire-drill protocols neutralize flashpoints before they escalate.
- Celebration calendars imprint joy and acknowledge milestones.
- Shared dashboards and retreats sustain momentum and inspire innovation.

Reflective Questions

1. What will your first "Blueprint Workshop" agenda include, and how will you schedule it this week?

2. Which three metrics will you display on your Shared Growth Dashboard, and why do they matter most?

3. How will you structure your Daily Three-Point Huddle to keep it under 5 minutes and powerfully aligned?

4. Describe a recent co-parenting friction and outline how you would apply the Fire-Drill Conflict Response.

5. What will your next Family Festival celebrate, and how will you invite your child to co-design it?

6. When and where will you hold your first Monthly Reflection and Recharge Retreat, and what question will guide your dialogue?

Conclusion

You have elevated co-parenting into a living system that restores your family from the ground up. Your **Family Restoration Blueprint** is now a dynamic, evolving map—uniting logistics, emotion, and celebration into one clear plan.

In Lesson 10, *Designing the Reconnection Plan,* you will crystallize these lessons into your personalized Reconnection Plan. You will set SMART goals, assign roles, and establish checkpoints—ensuring every strategy we have covered becomes your family's roadmap to lasting harmony and growth.

LESSON 10:
Designing the Reconnection Plan
A Structure Path Forward

Title & Purpose

A reunification strategy without structure stalls before it starts. In this lesson, you will translate the communication, connection, and co-parenting tools from Lessons 1–9 into a unified Reconnection Plan. You will learn how to set clear goals, map actionable steps, assign responsibilities, and establish metrics that keep your family's progress visible and on track. By the end, you will have a living document—your customized roadmap—that guides every decision and ensures sustainable, measurable reconnection.

What It Entails

- A framework for defining overarching goals and specific objectives
- Templates for timelines, milestones, and role assignments
- Guidelines for embedding communication protocols and bonding rituals
- A metric system to monitor progress and trigger course corrections
- Strategies for adaptation, maintenance, and long-term resilience

Why It Matters

- **Structured plans improve follow-through**: Families with a clear, documented roadmap are far more likely to stay on track and reach their reunification goals.

- **Visible milestones boost motivation**: Progress markers give parents and children something tangible to celebrate, keeping everyone engaged.

- **Clear role assignments reduce overlap and gaps**: When responsibilities are defined, confusion decreases and cooperation increases.

- **Embedded rituals anchor habits**: Regular check-ins and bonding activities create consistency and strengthen family bonds.

- **Ongoing metrics enable agility**: Weekly reviews and adjustment protocols help families adapt quickly and avoid getting stuck in repeating patterns.

Six Essential Elements of Your Reconnection Plan

1. **Define Clear Goals and Priorities**

- Identify 3-5 high-impact outcomes that matter most for your family's stability and healing (e.g., "Reduce transition-related stress," "Establish a consistent weekly family ritual," "Improve co-parent communication").

 • Rank them by urgency and impact to focus efforts where they matter most.

2. **Establish Timelines and Milestones**

   • Draft a timeline with major milestones (30-, 60-, and 90-day markers).

   • Attach measurable indicators (e.g., "First five empathy-pause successes," "Completion of initial Family Promise workshop").

3. **Allocate Roles And Responsibilities**

- Assign each task—scheduling check-ins, documenting rituals, leading evaluations—to a specific parent.

- Include back-up support (extended family, mentors) to cover gaps and ensure accountability.

4. **Integrate Communication Protocols and Rituals**

- Embed your chosen dialogue steps, open-ended check-ins, and bonding rituals into the plan's schedule.

- Define triggers for each (e.g., "Send structuring text 24 hours before a handoff," "Conduct Mood-Color drawing every Tuesday evening").

5. **Set Monitoring and Evaluation Metrics**

- Choose 4-6 quantitative and qualitative metrics (emotional-security scores, ritual adherence rate, reflective-journal entries).

 • Schedule regular reviews: weekly quick-checks, monthly deep dives, quarterly adjustments.

6. **Plan for Adaptation and Sustainability**

- Create an "Adjustment Protocol" outlining who initiates changes, how proposals are discussed, and how decisions are recorded.

- Build in periodic "reconnection retreats" or strategy sessions every 3-6 months to renew commitment and refresh tactics.

Common Pitfalls and Solutions

Goal-Setting

- **Pitfall:** Selecting too many objectives.
- **Solution:** Pare back to your top 2–3 SMART goals.

Timelines

- **Pitfall:** Deadlines slip by unnoticed.
- **Solution:** Automate calendar reminders and assign a "deadline buddy."

Roles and Responsibilities

- **Pitfall:** Duties overlap or get ignored.
- **Solution:** Use a shared digital chart (Google Sheets or Trello) with clear check-off steps.

Communication Protocols

- **Pitfall:** Messages go unacknowledged or misinterpreted.
- **Solution:** Agree on read-receipt protocols, priority tags, and a "cool-down" emoji.

Metrics and Reviews

- **Pitfall:** Data never gets reviewed.
- **Solution:** Embed metrics into your weekly check-in agenda with visual dashboards.

Adaptation

- **Pitfall:** The plan grows stale over time.
- **Solution:** Schedule quarterly "plan refresh" sessions and rotate the facilitator role.

Tools and Templates

- **Goal Worksheet:** SMART goal template with examples
- **Milestone Tracker:** 30/60/90-day Gantt chart
- **Role Matrix:** Color-coded responsibilities grid
- **Communication Protocol Doc:** Sample email/text templates + emoji legend
- **Metrics Dashboard:** Excel/Google Data Studio file with charts

- **Adjustment Protocol Flowchart:** Who, what, when for making changes

Accountability and Support Systems

- Accountability Partners: Pair each parent with a friend, coach, or therapist for monthly check-ins.

- Peer Cohort: Join a small group for bi-weekly "Reconnection Roundtables" to share wins and troubleshoot.

- Professional Checkpoint: Schedule a mid-term review with a reunification specialist or family counselor.

Technology Recommendations

- Shared Calendaring: Cozi or Google Calendar with color-coded events

- Task Management: Trello or Asana boards for roles + deadlines

- Check-In Reminders: Todoist recurring tasks or IFTTT automations

- Metrics and Surveys: Typeform or Google Forms for quick parent-child feedback

Customization Guidelines

- **Single-Parent vs. Parallel Parenting:** Adjust roles and checkpoints to fit solo or dual contexts.

- **Blended Families:** Expand the plan to include step-parents and co-parent teams of more than two.

- **Special-Needs Considerations:** Incorporate sensory breaks, visual schedules, or tailored communication cues.

- **Cultural and Faith-Based Rituals:** Integrate holidays, values, or spiritual practices that resonate with your family.

Implementation Checklist

1. Fill out and approve the Reconnection Plan document.
2. Schedule kickoff meeting and first weekly review.
3. Upload all templates to a shared drive or app.
4. Book accountability partner and professional checkpoint sessions.
5. Mark quarterly "Plan Refresh" sessions in everyone's calendars.

6. Launch your first Connection Check and record insights.

Next-Level Growth Path

• **Lesson 11:** Overcoming Setbacks—Staying Committed to the Journey

Fine-tuning metrics, leveraging feedback loops, and running A/B-style tests on your rituals.

• **Lesson 12:** Tracking Progress and Celebrating Milestones

Handling old patterns, deepening repair skills, and restoring harmony when challenges resurface.

• Optional Reconnection Mastermind

Join a cohort program for ongoing support, expert Q and A, and peer accountability.

Reflective Questions

1. Which two high-impact goals will you include in your plan, and why?

2. What are your first three milestones, and what metric will signal their achievement?

3. How will you divide responsibilities for timeline management, ritual facilitation, and evaluation?

4. Which communication triggers and bonding rituals will you schedule first?

5. What metrics and review cadence will you use to monitor progress?

6. How will your Adjustment Protocol function—who leads, what process, and how frequently?

Conclusion

You have done more than assemble goals, timelines, and metrics—you have laid the foundations for a living, breathing family ecosystem. This

Reconnection Plan is your compass and your heartbeat: a promise to your children that every step you take is intentional, every ritual purposeful, and every adjustment an act of love. As you track each milestone and honor each ritual, you will witness those first tremors of change—a calmer handoff, a shared laugh in the memory jar, a spark of pride when a goal is met.

Remember, a plan is only as good as the care you pour into it. Tend to it like a garden: nurture your new habits daily, prune what no longer serves you, and celebrate each bud of progress. Over time, those seeds of structure and ritual will blossom into lasting trust, resilience, and unity— transforming what once felt like enforced routines into the rhythms that sustain your family's bond.

In the next lesson, we will explore how to navigate unexpected challenges, recalibrate your indicators, and keep your Reconnection Plan adaptive and alive—so that every setback becomes a springboard for deeper connection.

PART IV – Maintaining the Journey

LESSON 11:
Weathering Setbacks

Staying Committed to the Process Turning Obstacles into Opportunities for Growth

Title & Purpose

Even the best Reconnection Plan faces hiccups. In this lesson, you will learn a five-step "Setback Response Process" that transforms cancellations, miscommunications, and emotional ruptures into catalysts for deeper trust. By the end, you will have tools to acknowledge disruptions, repair quickly, adapt your plan, and reinforce resilience—ensuring every obstacle fuels your family's growth.

Overview and Story Hook

These are fictional composites created for educational purposes. Any resemblance to real persons is coincidental.

The Martinez family's carefully crafted schedule unraveled when a holiday visit fell through at the last minute. Eight-year-old Sofia burst into tears, Dad lashed out in guilt, and Mom felt helpless. Rather than spiraling, they paused, applied their new Setback Response Process, and turned the meltdown into a teachable moment. Within hours, they would re-engaged Sofia with an impromptu "Comfort Movie Night," re-negotiated the schedule, and drafted a "Holiday Backup Plan." That evening, Sofia whispered, "Even when things go wrong, we fix them together."

The Martinez Family's Meltdown & Make-Good

Background

Sofia's eagerly anticipated holiday weekend was canceled due to Dad's work emergency.

Setback Response

1. **Acknowledge and validate**

   Mom knelt beside Sofia and said, "I know you feel disappointed—and that's okay."

2. **Rapid Repair Ritual**

They built a "Feelings Fort" with blankets and shared her favorite snacks.

3. **Adapt the Plan**

Dad rescheduled a special outing and sent a surprise video message.

4. **Growth Debrief**

Over dinner, they discussed what to do if plans change again.

5. **Celebrate Resilience**

Sofia earned a "Trouble-Shooter Star" on their Family Dashboard for her patience.

Results

Sofia's tears turned into laughter.

Both parents felt empowered instead of defeated.

The familys' trust deepened through collective problem-solving.

What It Entails and Five-Step Setback Response Process

1. **Immediate Acknowledgment and Validation**
- Technique: Pause all tasks. Use empathetic language: "I see this upset you, and I'm here."
- Drill: Practice a 30-second "Empathy Pause" when any frustration arises.
- Impact: Signals safety and prevents emotional escalation.
2. **Rapid Repair Ritual**
- **Technique:** Activate a pre-agreed "Comfort Plan" (snack, game, and story).
- **Drill:** Create a family list of five go-to rituals; practice one tonight.
- **Impact:** Quickly restores emotional equilibrium and reconnection.
3. **Root-Cause Analysis and Plan Adjustment**
- **Technique:** Ask "What happened?" and "What can we change?"
- **Drill:** Use a simple "Stop–Start–Continue" worksheet to capture insights.

- **Impact:** Turns disruption into actionable improvements for your Reconnection Plan.

4. **Leverage Setbacks for Growth**

- **Technique:** Invite your child to suggest one creative fix or ritual.
- **Drill:** During your next Weekly Lab Session, share setback learnings and vote on one family innovation.
- **Impact:** Empowers ownership and fosters a solution-oriented mindset.

5. **Reinforce Resilience and Celebrate Bounce-Back**

- **Technique:** Award a "Resilience Badge" on your Shared Dashboard or in your Family Promise Jar.

  Drill: After any repair, add a celebration note to your Family Festival calendar.

  Impact: Teaches children that setbacks are normal and overcome through teamwork. Age-Specific Adaptations

- **Littles (3–6):** Use emotion-face cards (happy/sad) to name feelings, then pick a comfort song together.
- **Elementary (7–10):** Co-create a "Setback Storybook" page illustrating the problem and solution.
- **Tweens (11–13):** Facilitate a short peer-style "Solution Brainstorm" where they lead suggestions.
- **Teens (14–17):** Offer private debrief options (voice note or text) before group repair.

Common Pitfalls and Course-Corrections

- Ritual list forgotten: Keep the five go-to rituals on the fridge or in a family chat pin.

- Analysis paralysis: Limit *Root-Cause* worksheet to one page and one core insight.

- Celebration fatigue: Alternate badge awards with simple verbal acknowledgments.

- Overwhelm: Scale back to one step at a time, starting with acknowledgment and validation.

Tools and Resources

- Family Promise Jar or Whiteboard for "Resilience Badge" notes
- "Stop–Start–Continue" printable worksheet (see Appendix)
- Shared family chat or pinned note for Comfort Plan rituals
- Emotion-face cards or simple visuals for littles
- Digital notes/voice-note app for teen debriefs

Next-Steps Checklist

- ☐ Practice a nightly Empathy Pause together
- ☐ Finalize your list of five go-to Rapid Repair rituals
- ☐ Complete a "Stop–Start–Continue" worksheet after your next setback
- ☐ Schedule a mini "Solution Brainstorm" in your Weekly Lab Session
- ☐ Add a Resilience Badge to your Shared Dashboard for today's repair
- ☐ Review and refine one Common Pitfall course-correction

Appendix: Setback Storybook and Worksheet

(Printable pages: "Stop–Start–Continue" worksheet, emotion-face cards template, Setback Storybook page layout)

Key Takeaways at a Glance

- Acknowledging emotions immediately prevents escalation.
- Rapid Repair Rituals restore safety and connection fast.
- Root-Cause Analysis turns problems into plan improvements.

- Involving your child sparks ownership and creativity.
- Celebration of resilience reinforces positive coping.

Reflective Questions

1. **Which step of the Setback Response Process will you practice first, and how?**

2. What new Rapid Repair Ritual will you introduce tonight?

3. How will you capture and apply insights from your next Root-Cause worksheet?

4. In what way can your child co-design a solution after the next setback?

5. How will you acknowledge and celebrate resilience when repair is complete?

Conclusion

You will now wield a robust resilience engine—complete with real-time response protocols, early warning metrics, accountability structures, and adaptive routines. Each setback you face becomes a strategic pivot point, not a dead end, ensuring your Reconnection Plan stays alive, responsive, and ever-progressing.

Next-Level Growth Path

Now that you have mastered turning setbacks into springboards, you are ready to evolve your Reconnection Plan into a self-sustaining family culture.

Lesson 12: Celebrating Wins — Transform small victories into lasting momentum by measuring achievements, scheduling routine reviews, and embedding joyful rituals.

Lesson 13: A Stronger Tomorrow —Evolve your family's culture through codified values, adaptive feedback loops, rotating leadership roles, and legacy celebrations.

Beyond the Workbook: Community and Support

Keep momentum high by tapping into peer forums, local workshops, or our Reconnection Mastermind for live Q and A, expert insights, and ongoing accountability.

LESSON 12:
Celebrating Wins
Tracking Progress G Milestones

Title & Purpose

Consistent reconnection depends on acknowledging every forward step. In this lesson, you will establish a robust progress-tracking system and celebration framework that turns small victories into sustained motivation. You will learn how to define meaningful metrics, schedule regular reviews, and embed celebration rituals so that each achievement, big or small, reinforces commitment and accelerates your family's journey.

Overview and Story Hook

These are fictional composites created for educational purposes. Any resemblance to real persons is coincidental.

After six weeks of weekly Connection Checks (5-minute co-parent check-in calls) and Memory Jar rituals (decorated containers for family members to drop positive memories), nine-year-old Lina's parents noticed flat engagement: check-in attendance dropped and the jar stayed empty. They introduced a simple "Milestone Map" on the fridge—tracking each completed ritual with a sticker and launched a Friday "High Five" moment to honor wins. Attendance soared back to 100%, and Lina started volunteering stories again. This lesson shows you how visible tracking and intentional celebrations reignite enthusiasm and reinforce positive habits.

What It Entails

- A framework for selecting and defining quantitative and qualitative metrics.

- Templates for progress dashboards, milestone maps, and celebration boards.

- Guidelines for scheduling reviews: weekly check-ins, monthly deep dives, quarterly celebrations.

- Strategies for designing age-appropriate celebration rituals.
- Best practices for publicly sharing achievements and reinforcing family pride.
- Adaptation tips for different family sizes and dynamics.

Why It Matters

Families that visually track progress are more consistent: Research on family engagement shows that visible tracking tools (dashboards, milestone maps) increase accountability and adherence to plans.

- **Celebrating small wins boosts co-parent engagement:** Studies highlight that recognizing even small steps forward strengthens motivation and keeps both parents invested.

- **Children thrive on positive recognition:** Regular acknowledgment of effort and progress builds emotional security and resilience, reducing anxiety tied to uncertainty.

- **Shared achievements strengthen trust.** When families celebrate progress together, it reduces stress and burnout while reinforcing a sense of unity.

- **Structured reviews keep families on track.** Regular check-ins and milestone reviews help prevent slippage, ensuring that goals stay visible and achievable.

Progress Tracking Framework

1. **Select Key Metrics**

- **Technique:** Choose 4–6 indicators—ritual completion rate, check-in consistency, child mood scores, shared activity frequency.

  - **Drill:** List your metrics with clear definitions and target thresholds.

  - **Impact:** Focuses attention on measurable progress rather than vague intentions.

2. **Build a Visual Dashboard**

- **Technique:** Use charts, sticker maps, or digital boards to display real-time data in a shared family space.

  - **Drill:** Create your dashboard template and post it where everyone can see.

  - **Impact:** Transforms abstract goals into tangible achievements.

3. **Schedule Regular Reviews**

- **Technique:** Embed metric reviews into your existing Connection Checks and co-parent meetings.

- **Drill:** Block recurring calendar slots—5 minutes weekly, 20 minutes monthly, 30 minutes quarterly.

  - **Impact:** Keeps progress front and center, preventing drift.

4. **Calibrate Goals and Milestones**

- **Technique:** Compare actual performance to targets, adjust thresholds, and add new milestones as needed.

  - **Drill:** After each monthly review, update your plan with revised dates and goals.
  - **Impact:** Ensures your plan evolves with your family's pace and priorities.

5. **Recognize and Celebrate Wins**

- **Technique:** Design rituals—sticker awards, "High Five" family huddle, celebratory treats—to honor completed milestones.

  - **Drill:** For each achieved metric, carry out its linked celebration within 24 hours.
  - **Impact:** Reinforces positive behavior and boosts collective morale.

6. **Share Achievements Publicly**

- **Technique:** Post updates on a shared family wall, group chat, or annual scrapbook. •

- **Drill:** Assign one parent the role of "Family Storyteller" to capture and share moments.

- **Impact:** Amplifies pride and accountability across the household.

Celebration Strategies

- **Sticker and Token Rewards**

  Example: Place one gold star sticker per completed ritual. At 10 stars, choose a family movie night.

- **Themed "Win Dinners"**

  Example Script: "This week our top milestone was ___________ let's celebrate with Lina's favorite tacos and share one highlight each."

- **Achievement Jar**

  Drop written notes of successes; read them aloud during monthly gatherings.

- **Family Star Spotlight**

  Rotate a "Family Star" each week—every member shares a personal win.

- **Creative Keepsakes**

  Craft milestone certificates or custom badges to commemorate progress.

Common Pitfalls and Solutions

Metric Overload

- **Pitfall:** Tracking too many indicators at once leads to confusion.
- **Fix:** Pare back to your top three metrics; add more only once those are stable.

  Dashboard Fatigue

- **Pitfall:** Family stops checking the board after a few weeks.
- **Fix:** Rotate who "hosts" the weekly review and refresh the visual every month.

  Celebration Drift

- **Pitfall:** Rituals become routine and lose their spark.
- **Fix:** Introduce a quarterly "surprise celebration" (new game, craft, or outing).

Data Gaps

- **Pitfall:** Missing entries in your tracker make reviews meaningless.
- **Fix:** Link metric updates to another anchor event (e.g., right after dinner).

  Budget Constraints

- **Pitfall:** Celebrations feel expensive or time-consuming.
- **Fix:** Lean into no-cost options—special shout-outs, homemade badges, or a family dance party.

- **Tools and Templates** Progress Dashboard Template (printable + digital) for a fill-in dashboard with columns Date, Ritual Completed (Y/N), Child Mood (1–5), and Notes.

- Milestone Map Sticker Sheet (with 30/60/90-day markers).

- Celebration Board Layout (DIY poster).

- Achievement Jar Labels and Journal Pages.

- Family Meeting Agenda (5-, 20-, and 30-minute versions).

Accountability and Support Systems

- **Accountability**: Buddy: Pair with a friend for monthly check-ins on metrics and wins.

- **Peer Pod:** Form a quarterly "Family Reconnection Roundtable" with 2–3 other co-parenting teams.

- **Professional Checkpoint**: Schedule a mid-lesson review with your reunification specialist to troubleshoot roadblocks.

Customization Guidelines

Different Ages

Young children: Use stickers and simple mood-faces.

Tweens/Teens: Offer choice in celebration rituals and let them co-lead reviews.

- **Family Structure**

Blended households: Create parallel dashboards for each sub-family and a joint main board.

Single parents: Build micro-celebrations around small daily rituals.

Cultural/Faith-Based Variations

Integrate holiday themes, values-driven awards, or faith rituals into your celebration calendar.

Implementation Checklist

1. Define your 4–6 key metrics.
2. Build and display your visual dashboard.
3. Block calendar slots for weekly, monthly, and quarterly reviews.
4. Set up your celebration board and gather supplies.
5. Assign your "Family Storyteller."
6. Schedule your first surprise quarterly celebration.

Final Reflection on the Plan

Nurturing your reunification plan is much like tending a garden: you sow intentions, water them with consistency, and prune away what no longer serves growth. In this reflection, you will harvest insights, cut back obstacles, and celebrate the resilience you have cultivated.

Practical Pruning Tips

- **Identify one or two rituals that feel stale. Ask:** "What small tweak could renew this for our family?"

- **Trim overly ambitious metrics.** If a weekly 30-minute check-in never lands, shorten it to 15 minutes or shift its timing.

- **Weed out negative language.** Turn "We failed to..." into "We noticed an opportunity to..."

Celebration Examples

- **Host a "Bloom Bash" after your next quarterly review:** lay out flowers or craft paper petals, each labeled with a win from the past three months.

- **Pruning Party:** pick one outdated ritual and jointly brainstorm its successor—treat the brainstorming like planting a new seedling.

- **Resilience Scroll:** create a simple scroll of ten "I am proud" statements gathered from every family member; read it aloud during a celebratory dinner.

Closing Reflection Question

How will you acknowledge and celebrate resilience in your family's journey, ensuring that each new shot of connection is honored and encouraged?

Conclusion

You have turned every small victory into shared pride and lasting momentum. By defining clear metrics, displaying progress on a visual dashboard, scheduling regular reviews, calibrating goals, and embedding celebration rituals, you have built an engine that keeps your family engaged and motivated. Achievement no longer fades into the background—each sticker, high-five, and spotlight moment reinforce your commitment and accelerates your journey toward deeper connection.

In the final lesson, you will codify this culture of celebration and accountability so it endures. You will define your family's core values, rotate leadership roles, design legacy celebrations, and embed adaptive feedback loops. These practices will transform your Reconnection Plan into a self-perpetuating family ethos—one that thrives long after you close this workbook.

LESSON 13:
A Stronger Tomorrow
Sustaining Growth beyond Reunion

Title & Purpose

You have built a living Reconnection Plan—now you will ensure it thrives long after this workbook closes. In Lesson 13, you will codify your family's core values, rotate leadership roles, design legacy celebrations, and embed adaptive feedback loops. These practices transform your plan into a self-perpetuating family ethos that continues to deepen trust, spark joy, and guide growth for years to come.

Overview and Story Hook

These are fictional composites created for educational purposes. Any resemblance to real persons is coincidental.

Two years after completing their Reconnection Plan, the Patel family noticed celebrations had become routine and their rituals felt stale. During a spring "Values Summit," their daughter Aisha declared, "I want our family to stand for courage, curiosity, and kindness." Inspired, they launched a rotating "Family President" role, created an annual "Courage Carnival," and added a "Lessons Learned" check-in at every dinner. Today, their home pulses with fresh energy, and each generation carries forward traditions that reflect their shared vision.

The Patel Family's Culture Evolution

Background

After Reunion, the Patels maintained their routines—but without a unifying purpose, engagement dipped.

Turning Point

They held a weekend Values Summit: every member—ages 6 to 42—named one value they cared about. They distilled three to live by, planned a calendar of legacy events, and agreed on quarterly leadership rotations.

Results

Family meetings tripled in participation. Sibling squabbles fell by 60%.

Grandma told neighbors: "I've never seen them more connected."

What It Entails and Five-Step Culture-Building Framework

1. Define Core Family Values

- **Technique:** Host a "Values Summit" where everyone proposes and votes on 3–5 guiding principles.

- **Drill:** Capture each value on cards; display them in your main gathering space.

- **Impact:** Aligns daily choices with a shared purpose and gives meaning to every ritual.

2. Rotate Leadership Roles

- **Technique:** Assign monthly "Family President" and "Chief Cheerleader" roles to different members.

- **Drill:** Create a simple role chart—outline responsibilities like running check-ins or planning treats.

- **Impact:** Builds ownership, nurtures leadership skills, and refreshes engagement.

3. Design Legacy Celebrations

- **Technique:** Invent annual or seasonal events— "Courage Carnival," "Gratitude Gala," or "Storytelling Solstice."

- **Drill:** Draft a one-page ceremony plan: theme, activities, symbols, and keepsakes.

- **Impact:** Anchors your values in memorable, multi-sensory experiences that bind generations.

4. Embed Adaptive Feedback Loops

- **Technique:** Add a "Lessons Learned" segment to each review—ask "What worked?" and "What's next?"

- **Drill:** Use feedback cards at dinner or in your digital dashboard; rotate the facilitator.

- **Impact:** Keeps your culture alive and evolving, letting you course-correct before habits stagnate.

Tap into Community and Mentorship

- **Technique:** Partner with another Reconnection family or join a local workshop for fresh ideas.

- **Drill:** Schedule quarterly peer-pod meetups or online mastermind sessions.

  Impact: Injects new perspectives, sustains accountability, and reminds you briefly are not alone.

Age-Specific Adaptations

- **Littles (3–6):** Illustrate values with storybooks and act them out in play.

- **Elementary (7–10):** Let them lead one monthly meeting and choose a legacy celebration theme.

- **Tweens (11–13):** Co-design feedback cards and manage digital dashboards.

- **Teens (14–17):** Rotate as peer-pod hosts and mentor younger siblings in leadership roles.

Common Pitfalls and Solutions

Values Drift

- **Pitfall:** Values cards get dusty on the wall.

- **Fix:** Rotate a "Value of the Month" to spotlight one principle in your rituals.

Leadership Fatigue

- **Pitfall:** Roles feel like chores.

- **Fix:** Keep role descriptions light—limit duties to 10–15 minutes per week.

Celebration Stagnation

- **Pitfall:** Annual events feel repetitive.

- **Fix:** Add a surprise element each year—guest speaker, new game, or collaborative art project.

Feedback Ignored

- **Pitfall:** Cards pile up without follow-through.

- **Fix:** Dedicate 5 minutes of your Weekly Check-in to read one card aloud and agree on one action.

Tools and Templates

- Values Summit Worksheet

- Leadership Role Chart

- Legacy Celebration Planner (one-page)

- Feedback Card Templates

- Peer-Pod Meetup Guide

Next-Steps Checklist

☐ Host your first Values Summit and capture the top 3–5 values.

☐ Assign and display leadership roles for the coming months.

☐ Draft one Legacy Celebration plan and set its date.

☐ Update your review agenda with a Lessons Learned segment.

☐ Reach out to one other Reconnection family for a peer-pod session.

Reflective Questions

1. Which three values will guide your family's culture, and why do they matter?

2. Who will serve as "Family President" next month, and what will they lead?

3. What theme and activities will your first Legacy Celebration include?

4. How will you gather and act on adaptive feedback in your next review?

5. Which external community or mentor will you connect with to sustain your momentum?

Conclusion

You began this journey at the edge of fractured bonds and, through thirteen transformative lessons, have built a self-sustaining family culture rooted in trust, creativity, and shared purpose. Now it is time to honor what you have achieved and ignite excitement for what comes next.

A Brief Journey Recap

- **Part I – Foundations of Reconnection (Lessons 1–3)**: You confronted the cost of separation, discovering why reconnection matters, and grounding yourself in the principles of healing—hope, accountability, and daily courage.

- **Part II – The Blueprint Framework (Lessons 4–7)**: You prepared the ground with self-reflection and readiness tools, built bridges through communication rituals and scripts, faced barriers like anger and mistrust with practical exercises, and established daily acts of reconnection through journaling and family rituals.

- **Part III – Tools for Families & Professionals (Lessons 8–10)**: You explored exercises for parents and children, gained guidance for therapists, social workers, and advocates, and drew inspiration from case studies and stories of hope.

- **Part IV – Sustaining the Journey (Lessons 11–13)**: You learned to prevent relapse into conflict, created a unifying family vision statement, and embraced a legacy of reconnection—passing healing forward to future generations.

Families who embrace these strategies consistently report stronger adherence to their commitments, greater co-parent engagement, and meaningful gains in their children's sense of security and trust.

Graduation Ceremony Rituals

Family Reunion Gala

- Host a "graduation" dinner.

- Print Certificates of Mastery for each member.

- Read aloud your 3–5 Core Values and have everyone share a one-sentence vow for the year ahead.

Legacy Toolkit

- **Time Capsule:** Write letters to your future selves and decide when to open them.
- **Family Storybook:** Gather photos and mementos into an album or digital slideshow.
- **Video Montage:** Record 30-second clips of "My proudest moment" and edit in CapCut or iMovie.

Next-Lesson Launch

- Introduce a new Legacy Celebration for next quarter (e.g., Courage Carnival, Gratitude Gala).

- Invite friends, neighbors, or a peer-pod to join your community of reconnection.

Final Flourish and Call to Action

This workbook may end here, but your stronger tomorrow is just beginning. Carry your Core Values every day, keep your Time Capsule sealed until its reveal, and continue co-creating your family's story with intention and joy.

Optional Next Step: Join the Reconnection Mastermind for live Q and A, expert workshops, and peer accountability to keep this epic journey blazing.

Disclosure on Illustrative Stories

Dear Reader, before you turn the page to our heartfelt acknowledgments, I want to be transparent about the narratives woven throughout this workbook. Every family name, case study, and personal anecdote—from the Martinezes to the Patels to the Nguyens—is a fictional composite created for illustration. These stories do not depict real individuals or actual court cases.

Rather, they are dramatized examples designed to bring the lessons to life, highlight common challenges, and spark your own creative thinking about how to apply these strategies in your family's unique context. Any resemblance to actual persons, living or deceased, is purely coincidental.

Our goal in using these vignettes is to provide vivid, relatable scenarios that respect confidentiality while demonstrating how the principles in this workbook can transform real-world situations.

Acknowledgments

Divine Guidance

Above all, I give thanks to the guiding presence that inspired every insight in this Blueprint. When the path felt clouded by doubt, that quiet assurance reminded me that change is always possible and hope never abandons us.

To the Families

To the families who have dared to walk the jagged edge of separation and then reach across the divide—your bravery, honesty, and relentless hope have forged the heart of this work. You taught me that reconnection is not a destination but a daily act of courage, and every story you shared became the spark for these pages.

To the Professionals

To the therapists, social workers, and advocates whose compassion lights the way through every storm—your unwavering clarity, fierce dedication, and refusal to settle for sufficient have inspired every exercise and prompt in this Blueprint. You remind the world that healing is possible when we hold one another with both empathy and accountability.

To my mentors and collaborators

Those who pushed me beyond my comfort zone, challenged each chapter to shine with purpose, and believed in these tools before they even existed— thank you for refining every sentence, every lesson, and every symbol until it pulsed with potential.

To My Family & Friends

To my wife, our children, and grandchild—your laughter, late-night encouragement, and steadfast belief in my vision have been my anchor and the wind at my back.

To the rest of my family and to every friend who reminded me to remember your "why" when doubt's voice grew louder—your love in every season of this journey has made this Blueprint possible.

A Final Word

My Family Reconnection Blueprint is more than ink on paper. It is a rallying cry to keep families out of court, to mend what was torn, and to reunify hearts one deliberate step at a time. May these tools, instructions, and prompts refocus the lives you cherish most and light a path of hope for every household that dares to begin again.

With gratitude beyond measure.

RESOURCES & REFERENCES

Books

- The Whole-Brain Child – Daniel J. Siegel & Tina Payne Bryson
- Nonviolent Communication – Marshall B. Rosenberg
- Families in Transition: Parenting After Divorce – Philip M. Stahl
- The Seven Principles for Making Marriage Work – John Gottman

Organizations

- National Family Resiliency Center (NFRC) – Counseling, mediation, and family transition support
- American Association for Marriage and Family Therapy (AAMFT) – Directory of licensed family therapists
- National Council on Family Relations (NCFR) – Research and education on family well-being
- Children's Bureau (U.S. Dept. of Health & Human Services) – Programs supporting child welfare and family stability
- National Family Support Network (NFSN) – Community-based family support programs

Hotlines (U.S.-based)

- National Parent Helpline – 1-855-427-2736
- Childhelp National Child Abuse Hotline – 1-800-422-4453
- National Domestic Violence Hotline – 1-800-799-7233
- SAMHSA Helpline – 1-800-662-4357

Websites

- Child Welfare Information Gateway – https://www.childwelfare.gov/
- Gottman Institute – https://www.gottman.com/
- Sesame Workshop Parenting Resources – https://www.sesameworkshop.org/
- APA Division of Family Psychology – https://www.apa.org/about/division/div43
- National Family Support Network – https://www.nfsn.org/

GLOSSARY

Core Values – The guiding principles your family commits to living by each day. They serve as anchors during times of conflict and celebration.

Time Capsule – A sealed record of your family's commitments, reflections, or hopes, to be opened at a future date as a way to celebrate growth and reconnection.

Accountability Ritual – A structured practice designed to help family members take responsibility for their actions, repair trust, and restore balance.

Reconnection Mastermind – A live community space offering Q&A, expert workshops, and peer accountability to support ongoing healing beyond this workbook.

Milestone Map – A visual tool for tracking progress, celebrating achievements, and keeping the family focused on shared goals.

Celebration Board – A communal space (physical or symbolic) where families highlight victories, big or small, to reinforce connection and joy.

BOOKS BY JESSIE MIKES

1. **Anger Unchained** (Upcoming)

   A transformative exploration of anger, accountability, and healing...

2. **Hold the Middle** (Upcoming)

   A powerful guide to navigating family dynamics and finding balance...

   My Family Reconnection Blueprint

   You are currently reading this workbook, designed to rebuild trust, repair relationships, and foster reconnection...

ABOUT THE AUTHOR

Jessie Mikes is an author, group facilitator, reunification visitation professional, and the founder of JLMS Provider of Family Services. Through transformative workbooks, rituals, and branded resources, Jessie equips families and professionals with tools to rebuild trust, foster accountability, and reconnect with hope.

With a gift for blending emotional storytelling and structured guidance, Jessie's work emphasizes empathy, resilience, and practical strategies that keep families out of court and united in healing. Their projects—including Anger Unchained, Hold the Middle (upcoming), and My Family Reconnection Blueprint—form a growing collection of resources designed to inspire lasting change.

Beyond the pages, Jessie finds grounding in family dinners, sunrise journaling, and the joy of living alongside their wife, children, and grandchild in Southern California. The memory of Jessie's late brother, Ajabu, is honored throughout their work as a guiding light and reminder that reconnection is always possible. Every lesson, ritual, and exercise carries forward that legacy of courage, repair, and love.

INVITATION TO CONNECT

This Blueprint is just the beginning. If you'd like to continue the journey, I invite you to connect with me and the JLMS community:

- **Website** – Visit [jlmsproviderfamilyservicesllc.com] for bonus tools, downloadable resources, and updates on upcoming projects.

- **Newsletter** – Subscribe for insights, new rituals, and exclusive content delivered straight to your inbox.

- **Email** – Reach me directly at [jessie@jlmsfamcoaching.com] for professional inquiries, collaborations, or personal reflections.

- **QR Code** – Scan to access a library of worksheets, video guides, and community events.

- **Social Media** – Follow JLMS Blueprints on Instagram, Facebook,

LinkedIn, and YouTube for daily inspiration, behind-the-scenes updates, and live conversations.

•	**Community Group** – Join the Reconnection Mastermind for live Q&A, expert workshops, and peer accountability to keep your family's journey blazing.

Together, we can keep building stronger tomorrows—one deliberate step at a time.